Grill Kitchen

Keto BBQ Cookbook

Simple Yet Tasty Keto BBQ Recipes
Fresh from Your Backyard Grill or
Kitchen

Table of Contents

Introduction

Many persons around the world have discovered the Ketogenic diet and have testified that this special lifestyle is a very healthy one and have totally recommended it.

Maybe you have been trying many other diets that are not working for you, maybe you have also tried some of the starvation diets that promised instant results and have even tried fasting, but you can't keep up with the meal skipping. Don't give up just yet, try the Ketogenic diet – proven scientifically to aid in the burning of fat, loss of weight and provides much more.

Also referred to as the Keto Diet, this is a high-fat, low-carb diet. This food program forces the body in a different metabolic state where the fat that is burned, instead of glucose it is burned as energy.

in short, this Keto BBQ Cookbook will not only introduce the Ketogenic diet to you, but it will also provide you with some tasty, delicious barbecue dishes that will help you burn fat, lose weight and help you gain other great benefits for your health overall.

Slow-Cooker Barbecue Ribs

These delicious ribs will knock your boots off.

Serves: 2

Time: 4 hrs. 10 mins.

Ingredients:

- 1lb. pork ribs
- Pink salt
- Freshly ground black pepper
- 1.25 oz. package dry rib-seasoning rub
- ½ cup sugar-free barbecue sauce

Directions:

1. With the crock insert in place, preheat your slow cooker to high.

2. Generously season the pork ribs with pink salt, pepper, and dry rib-seasoning rub.

3. Stand the ribs up along the walls of the slow-cooker insert, with the bonier side facing inward.

4. Pour the barbecue sauce on both sides of the ribs, using just enough to coat.

5. Cover, cook for 4 hours and serve.

Bacon Wrapped Scallops on The Grill

These Bacon Wrapped Scallops makes the perfect Keto snack.

Serves: 4

Time: 30 mins.

Ingredients:

- 12 bacon slices
- 12 large scallops
- Garlic to taste
- Pinch onion powder

- Pinch paprika
- Cayenne pepper to taste
- Salt and pepper to taste
- Melted butter

Directions:

1. Preheat your grill for medium-high heat. Preheat your oven to 375 degrees.

2. Transfer your bacon to your tray to form a single layer. Bake 9-12 minutes until partially cooked but still pliable.

3. Season the scallops with the garlic, onion powder, paprika, cayenne pepper, salt and pepper.

4. Wrap scallops with bacon then thread onto skewers.

5. Grill 6-8 minutes to desired doneness, turning often. Brush with the melted butter and serve.

Grilled Pork Tenderloins

Enjoy these tenderloins for either lunch or dinner.

Serves: 4

Time: 25 mins.

Ingredients:

- 2 pound pork tenderloin
- Pinch rosemary, garlic powder and onion powder
- Salt and pepper to taste
- 1 tablespoon olive oil

Directions:

1. Rub the seasonings, salt and pepper into the tenderloin. Brush with the olive oil.

2. On the grill, sear all sides and move to a less hot part of the grill.

3. Cover and cook, turning occasionally. Cut into medallions and serve.

Low Carb Grilled Broccoli Cauliflower Salad

Cauliflower and Broccoli are both low in carbs, making it the perfect accompaniment to any entrée.

Serves: 6

Time: 30 mins.

Ingredients:

- 1 cup broccoli florets
- 1 cup cauliflower florets

- 1/4 cup olive oil
- Pinch garlic powder
- Salt and pepper to taste
- 1 cup shredded Boar's Head Pecorino Romano Cheese

Directions:

1. Prepare your grill on high heat. Drizzle your cauliflower and broccoli with the olive oil, then season with pepper, salt and garlic powder. Toss to coat.

2. Transfer to grill basket and grill till slightly charred.

3. Toss with cheese then serve.

Grilled King Crab

For a luxurious snack these delicious King Crab.

Serves: 2

Time: 15 mins.

Ingredients:

- 1/2 cup olive oil
- 1/2 cup butter
- 4 pounds crab legs

Directions:

1. Mix together the olive oil and butter. Brush the mixture all over the legs.

2. Cook the crab on a grill over medium-high heat, 3 minutes on each side. Serve with clarified butter.

Low Carb Barbecue Pulled Pork

This low carb Low Carb Barbecue Pulled Pork is perfect for sandwiches. Be sure to read the label of the BBQ sauce to ensure it is Keto approved.

Serves: 18

Time: 10 hrs. 10 mins.

Ingredients:

- 5 pound pork shoulder or pork butt
- 1/2 cup, sliced onion
- 4 garlic cloves, minced

- 1 cup chicken or beef broth
- 1 teaspoon brown sugar
- 1 teaspoon chili powder
- 1 teaspoon ground cumin
- 1/2 teaspoon ground cinnamon
- Salt and pepper to taste
- 2 cups Zero or Low Carb Barbecue Sauce (optional)

Directions:

1. You might notice the brown sugar in the recipe. Normally, I wouldn't put sugar into a low-carb meal, but I think just a small amount of sugar here can go a really long way to the flavor.

2. Place all ingredients into slow cooker on low for 8-10 hours. When finished cooking, remove any bones and cut or shred into small chunks, then return to Slow cooker.

3. Quick and easy, right? For a great serving suggestion, use some fresh lettuce as a wrap for the pork. Crisp and crunchy meets soft and spicy!

Grilled Parmesan Encrusted Tilapia

This parm encrusted Tilapia is fit for any event.

Serves: 4

Time: 40 mins.

Ingredients:

- 1/2 cup olive oil
- 1 cup shredded parmesan cheese
- Pinch garlic powder
- Pinch onion powder

- Pinch paprika
- Salt and pepper to taste
- 4-6 tilapia fillets

Directions:

1. Place the olive oil in a dish. Combine the pepper, salt, paprika, onion powder, garlic powder and parmesan cheese in another dish then mix well.

2. Dip the fillets in the oil and press into the cheese mixture, coating both sides. Preheat your grill for medium-high heat.

3. Place the fillets on a grill pan and grill 9-11 minutes per side to desired doneness.

Smoked Pork Butt

Throw your slab of porkbutt on your grill and enjoy the smokey flavors of this delicious recipe.

Serves: 8

Time: 9 hrs.

Ingredients:

- Hickory wood chips, soaked
- 4-5 pound pork butt roast
- Pinch garlic powder
- Pinch onion powder

- Salt and pepper to taste
- Melted butter

Directions:

1. Prepare the smoker to 225 to 250 degrees and add the soaked chips. Rinse the pork butt and pat dry.

2. Season with the pepper, onion powder, salt and garlic powder. Place in a large disposable roasting pan and place in the smoker.

3. Keep your smoker temp at 225 to 250 degrees adding coals and chips as needed. Smoke for 7-9 hours until desired doneness (160 degrees internal temp) basting every hour with the butter.

Low Carb Grilled Fajitas

These Low Carb Grilled Fajitas some of the handiest things you can have for grilling.

Serves: 2

Time: 35 mins.

Ingredients:

- 1 pound flank steak, cut into strips
- 1/2 cup sliced onions
- 1/2 green bell pepper, sliced

- 1/4 cup olive oil
- Salt, pepper, and Pinch garlic powder
- Pinch garlic and onion powder
- Pinch taco seasoning

Directions:

1. In a Ziploc bag place the steak and the vegetables in another. Whisk the remaining ingredients together and evenly pour into the bags.

2. Close and refrigerate 1-2 hours, turning occasionally. Prepare a grill for medium-high heat, place all ingredients in a grill basket and grill to desired doneness.

Bacon and Cheese Stuffed Burgers on the Grill

These burgers are packed with juicy Keto goodness.

Serves: 4

Time: 25 mins.

Ingredients:

- 8 slices bacon, cooked and crumbled
- 1 cup grated sharp cheddar cheese
- 2 pounds ground beef
- Pinch garlic powder
- Pinch onion powder

- Salt and pepper to taste

Directions:

1. Mix the bacon and cheese in a medium bowl; set aside. Form the beef into 8 patties and season with the garlic powder, onion powder, salt and pepper.

2. Roll the cheese mixture into 4 balls and place onto four patties. Place the remaining four patties on top, press and seal the edges.

3. Place in the freezer while preparing the grill. Preheat a grill for medium-high heat. Grill the burgers to desired doneness.

Low Carb Jalapeno Poppers

Jalapeno poppers are perfect as appetizers or snacks.

Serves: 16

Time: 20 mins.

Ingredients:

- 8 large jalapeno peppers
- 4 ounces cream cheese, softened
- 4 ounces sharp cheddar cheese

- 8 slices bacon, cooked and crumbled
- Pinch garlic powder

Directions:

1. Preheat grill for medium-high. Remove the tops of the peppers with a knife and deseeds and remove membrane without cutting the pepper in half.

2. Combine the cream cheese, cheddar cheese, bacon and garlic in a mixing bowl and mix well.

3. Stuff each pepper with the mixture and thread onto skewers. Grill until nice and charred to desired doneness.

Blue Crabs on the Grill

These delicious crabs are great for a backyard BBQ.

Serves: 2

Time: 20 mins.

Ingredients:

- 2 sticks butter
- Pinch salt, pepper, and Pinch garlic powder
- 1 tablespoon old bay seasoning
- 6 cleaned blue crabs

Directions:

1. Mix in the seasonings in the melted the butter. Brush the crabs all over with the mixture and transfer to a grill on medium-high flame.

2. On each side cook for 6 minutes or to desired doneness. Transfer to a plate and serve.

Low Carb Cilantro Lime Chicken

This delicious marinated chicken is grilled to perfection and deliciously smoky.

Serves: 6

Time: 30 mins.

Ingredients:

- 1 cut-up chicken
- 1/4 cup olive oil
- 1/4 cup fresh lime juice

- 1/4 cup chopped cilantro
- Red pepper flakes to taste
- Salt and pepper to taste

Directions:

1. Choose a suitable shallow dish for marinating then place the chicken in it. Whisk the rest of ingredients together and pour over the chicken.

2. Cover and refrigerate overnight, turning occasionally. Prepare your grill for medium-high heat. Grill about an hour to desired doneness, turning occasionally.

3. You can bake 20 minutes per side on 350 degrees to cut down on the cooking time.

Super Spicy Steak Kebobs

These Kabobs are fit for a king.

Serves: 8

Time: 18 mins.

Ingredients:

- flank steak, 2 lbs., cut into strips
- 1/2 cup low carb soy sauce
- 1/2 cup olive oil
- 2-3 tablespoons sugar free molasses
- 1-2 teaspoon cayenne pepper
- Pinch garlic powder
- Pinch onion powder

- Pinch ginger

Directions:

1. Place the steak in a large Zip Loc Bag. Whisk the remaining ingredients together in a small bowl and pour into the bag. Seal the bag and shake to coat.

2. Place in the refrigerator and marinate overnight, turning occasionally.

3. Preheat a grill for medium-high heat. Thread the beef onto skewers and grill to desired doneness.

Grilled Bacon Wrapped Shrimp

Shrimp and bacon complement each other perfectly in this delicious snack.

Serves: 1

Time: 15 mins.

Ingredients:

- Half as many strips of bacon as there are shrimp
- 1/4 pound (or more) shrimp, peeled and de-veined
- Pinch garlic powder
- Salt and pepper to taste

- Olive oil for brushing

Directions:

1. Cook the bacon so it is browned yet pliable. Season the shrimp and brush with the olive oil.

2. Cut all bacon strip in half and wrap around the shrimps, securing with toothpicks.

3. Skewer the shrimp if desired and cook on the grill over medium-high heat to desired doneness.

Low Carb Veggie Grill

Nothing brightens up a barbeque dinner than a spread of fresh grilled vegetables.

Serves: 4

Time: 45 mins.

Ingredients:

- 1/2 cup olive oil, divided
- 1/4 cup balsamic vinegar

- 2 garlic cloves, minced
- Italian herbs to taste
- Salt and pepper to taste
- Your choice of low carb veggies like:
- Asparagus, trimmed
- Bell peppers, de-seeded and halved
- Broccoli, cut into florets
- Cauliflower, cut into florets
- Eggplants, thickly sliced
- Mushrooms, whole
- Yellow Squash, sliced lengthwise
- Zucchini

Directions:

1. Prepare the grill for medium-high heat. Whisk 1/4 cup of the oil together with the vinegar, vinegar, garlic, herbs, salt and pepper; set aside.

2. Brush the remaining olive oil on the vegetables and coat lightly. Grill the vegetables until tender and lightly charred all over.

Bacon Wrapped Filet Mignon on The Grill

This slab of deliciousness is perfect at any level of doneness,

Serves: 1

Time: 20 mins.

Ingredients:

- 2 strips bacon
- 1 filet Mignon steak
- Pinch salt, pepper, onion powder, and garlic powder

Directions:

1. In a frying pan, cook the bacon until it is brown but pliable.

2. Season the filet, then wrap the bacon strips around it. Secure with kitchen twine. Place the steak on the grill, heated to medium-high.

3. Cook to desired doneness, remove the twine, and serve.

Beef Kabobs

These tasty kabobs are simple to whip up and tasty.

Serves: 2

Time: 18 mins.

Ingredients:

- 1/2 pound beef filet or sirloin, cut into bite-sized pieces
- Pinch onion and garlic powder
- Salt and pepper to taste
- 1 tablespoon butter, melted

Directions:

1. Season the steak pieces. Spear them on a metal skewer. Brush with the butter, then place on a grill on medium-high heat.

2. Cook to desired doneness, then transfer to a plate and serve.

Low Carb Barbecue Baby Back Ribs

These delicious ribs can be found on many take out menus but this specific recipe with a twist will be coming from your kitchen.

Serves: 8

Time: 3 hrs. 10 mins.

Ingredients:

- 2 racks pork baby back ribs
- 1 teaspoon garlic powder
- 1 teaspoon onion powder

- 1 teaspoon chili powder
- Cayenne pepper to taste (optional)
- 1 teaspoon old bay seasoning
- 1 teaspoon rubbed thyme
- Salt and pepper to taste

Directions:

1. Place the ribs on a clean working surface. Combine the remaining ingredients to make a rub and mix well. Rub your spice all over the ribs, cover and refrigerate overnight.

2. Place in a baking sheet, cover with aluminum foil and bake on 250 degrees for 2 hours. Prepare a grill for medium-high flame and grill the ribs 30-40 minutes, turning occasionally.

3. Brush with low carb barbecue sauce during the last 20 minutes if desired.

Grilled Bacon Wrapped Chicken

The bacon featured in this recipe will ooze delicious fat into the chicken breast.

Serves: 1

Time: 35 mins.

Ingredients:

- 4 strips bacon
- 1 boneless chicken breast

- Salt and pepper to taste
- Pinch of garlic and onion powder
- 1 tablespoon olive oil

Directions:

1. Cook the bacon so it is browned yet pliable. Season the chicken, brush it with oil, and wrap it with the bacon, securing it with kitchen twine if needed.

2. Cook on the grill to desired doneness over medium-high heat. Remove the twine and serve.

Barbecue Chicken

This classic barbecue dish is perfect with a side of cole slaw.

Serves: 6

Time: 25-30 mins.

Ingredients:

- 1 whole chicken, cut up
- 2 tablespoons olive oil

- Salt, pepper, garlic powder, and Pinch onion powder
- Zero or low carb barbecue sauce (optional)

Directions:

1. Rinse the chicken and pat dry. Combine all other ingredients, except for the sauce, and brush over the chicken.

2. Pre-cook in the oven for an hour at 300 degrees. Preheat a grill for medium-high heat. Grill the chicken 12-15 minutes to desired doneness, turning often.

3. If using sauce, brush it over the chicken during the last 20 minutes.

Cheesy Oysters on the Grill

If you like delicacies, you will love these grilled oysters.

Serves: 4

Time: 20 mins.

Ingredients:

- 2 dozen oysters on the half shell
- 2-3 tablespoons melted butter

- Pinch garlic powder
- 1/2 cup parmesan cheese

Directions:

1. Preheat your grill for high heat. Drizzle the butter over the oysters, sprinkle with the garlic powder and parmesan cheese and grill until the oysters begin to curl. Serve immediately.

Flank Steak on the Grill

Here we have yet another traditional plate of goodness.

Serves: 2

Time: 20 mins.

Ingredients:

- 1 pound flank steak
- Pinch garlic and onion powder

- Salt and pepper to taste

Directions:

1. Season the steak. Place it on the grill on medium-high heat.

2. Cook to desired doneness, let sit, slice against the grain and serve.

Barbecue Pork Chops

Nothing screams barbecue like a juicy pork chop.

Serves: 2

Time: 20 mins.

Ingredients:

- 2 pork chops
- Pinch salt, pepper, paprika, garlic powder and onion powder
- 1 tablespoon olive oil

- Zero-carb barbecue sauce (optional)

Directions:

1. Season the pork chops and brush them with the olive oil. Place them on the grill at medium-high heat and cook to desired doneness, about 10 minutes.

2. If using sauce, brush with the sauce and cook for 3-5 additional minutes.

Grilled Bacon Burger

Beef wrapped in crisp bacon and cooked in its succulent juices equals nothing short of perfection.

Serves: 1

Time: 20 mins.

Ingredients:

- 3 strips bacon
- 1/4 pound (or more) ground beef
- Pinch of garlic and onion powder
- Salt and pepper

Directions:

1. Cook the bacon until it is browned yet pliable. Season the beef and form it into a patty. Wrap the bacon around the burger, securing it with kitchen twine if needed.

2. Cook the burger on the grill over medium-high heat to desired doneness. Serve with mayonnaise and mustard.

Chicken Kabobs

These chicken skewers are simply seasoned but they carry a delicious punch of flavor.

Serves: 2

Time: 25 mins.

Ingredients:

- chicken breast, 1/2 pound (cut into bite-sized)
- Dash garlic powder

- Salt and pepper to taste
- 1 tablespoon butter, melted

Directions:

1. Season the chicken pieces. Spear them on a metal skewer. Brush with the butter, then place on a grill on medium-high heat.

2. Cook to desired doneness, then transfer to a plate and serve.

Barbecue Pulled Beef

This tasty pulled beef recipe is perfect for sandwiches or over a serving of rice.

Serves: 12

Time: 8 -10 hrs.

Ingredients:

- 4-5 pound chuck roast
- 2 yellow onions, sliced or diced
- 2 garlic cloves, minced

- 1 cup chicken or beef broth
- 1 tablespoon artificial brown sugar sweetener
- Pinch chili powder
- Pinch ground cumin
- Pinch ground cinnamon
- Salt and pepper to taste
- 2 cups zero or low carb barbecue sauce (optional)

Directions:

1. Place all ingredients into slow cooker on low for 8-10 hours.

2. When finished cooking, remove any bones and cut or shred into small chunks, then return to slow cooker.

Devilled Eggs

Deviled eggs are easy to whip up but intricate enough to serve at the most elite events.

Serves: 6

Time: 18 mins.

Ingredients:

- 6 boiled eggs, peeled
- 1/4 cup mayonnaise
- 1 teaspoon yellow mustard
- 1 teaspoon vinegar or hot sauce
- Salt and pepper to taste

Directions:

1. Cut the eggs in half lengthwise. In a bowl, place the yolks and the other ingredients.

2. Mix thoroughly. Spoon the mixture into the egg halves. Garnish with paprika.

Low Carb Barbecue Spareribs

If you love cooking on the grill or the delicious aromas this Sparerib is about to take you to heaven.

Serves: 4

Time: 8 hrs.

Ingredients:

- 4 pounds spareribs
- 1/2 cup chopped onions
- 1 clove garlic, minced
- 1 teaspoon liquid smoke

- Salt and pepper to taste
- Zero-carb barbecue sauce (optional)

Directions:

1. In the slow cooker, place all ingredients except for sauce, if using it. Cook on low for 8 hours.

2. If using barbecue sauce, transfer ribs to a grill on medium-high heat.

3. Brush with the sauce and cook until caramelized, about 5 minutes or less.

Barbecue Smoked Turkey Legs

Give Thanksgiving a twist with these delicious BBQ Smoked Turkey Legs.

Serves: 2

Time: 6 hrs.

Ingredients:

- Hickory wood chips, soaked
- 2 turkey legs
- Pinch garlic powder
- Pinch onion powder or to taste

- Salt and pepper to taste
- Melted butter

Directions:

1. Heat your smoker to 225 to 250 degrees and add the soaked chips. Rinse the turkey legs and pat dry. Season with the salt, garlic powder, onion powder and pepper.

2. Place the legs in a large disposable roasting pan and place in the smoker. Keep your smoker temp at 225 to 250 degrees adding coals and chips when.

3. Smoke for 4-6 hours until desired doneness (180 degrees internal temp) basting every hour with the butter.

Conclusion

Thank you for taking the time out to read through my Grill Kitchen Style Keto BBQ Cookbook. I hope you enjoyed all 30 simple yet tasty keto BBQ recipes fresh from your backyard grill or kitchen. The Keto journey is such a fun and fulfilling road to walk and it helps a ton when you can share it with your friends and loved ones.

If you liked what you read through, please take some time to leave me a review on Amazon.

See you soon.